夜虎出林

Tiger in the Moonlight
Copyright © 2004
By Paul Koh
ISBN: 0-9755201-0-5
LCCN: 2004108911

All rights reserved.
No part of this book may be reproduced
or transmitted in any form, language or by
any means without written permission
from the publisher.

Printed in Hong Kong
Second Edition 2004

Published by
Bo Law Kung Fu Federation
385 Broadway. Suite 3R.
New York, N.Y. 10013

Art Direction. *Tak Wah Eng*
Design. *Spencer Bagley*
Photography. *Spencer Bagley*

TIGER *in the* MOONLIGHT
Classical Kung Fu Forms and Matching Set

Paul Koh

Acknowledgements

I wish to sincerely thank Master Tak Wah Eng for his knowledge, guidance and support. My gratitude and appreciation is also extended to Andre Bowen for his assistance in executing the techniques in this book. To Spencer Bagley, I express my gratitude for his tireless effort in designing this publication.

Forward by Master Tak Wah Eng

The Five Animal System of Kung Fu is an art both fascinating and esoteric, and any venture seeking to capture it, to translate its inherent physicality into a purely written form, is a daunting task. With the Five Animal Kung Fu Matching Set Series, Sifu Paul Koh has applied his decades of knowledge and experience to compose a volume that expertly brings to life on the page what a student would typically learn only in person. For anyone without any background in Kung Fu, but with an abiding interest in its traditional artistry, philosophy, and fundamental skills, the Five Animal System is an excellent introduction that I could not recommend more strongly.

"The tiger roars with spiritual power."
"His energy sweeps over mountains and rivers."

CONTENTS

Five Animal Kung Fu..2

Tiger Form..6
    Form #1..12
    Form #2..24

Moonlight Tiger Matching Set..................................34

About the Author..60

少林五形拳 FIVE ANIMAL KUNG FU

The history of the Shaolin Temple and its style of Kung Fu are steeped in many legends. Today renowned all over the world, Shaolin is and has been justly famous for contributing greatly to the advancement of the Chinese martial arts; but its import as a spiritual center is just as notable in as much as Shaolin is the birthplace of "Chan" or Zen Buddhism, the most widely known and practiced branch of the religion.

During the northern Wei Dynasty, in the early 6th century, an Indian monk commonly known by the Sanskrit title Bodhidharma (or as pronounced in Cantonese, Dat Mor) journeyed to China to spread a form of Buddhism based on the Lankavatara Sutra, which emphasizes meditation toward the raising of personal consciousness above scripture or doctrine. Eventually settling in the Shaolin Temple, already a Buddhist site, he began to preach his religious philosophy as well as train the monks' in a particular form of basic exercise, the "law horn gung" or Buddha's exercise. The techniques Dat Mor brought to Shaolin were originally designed to strengthen the body and alleviate the stress and pressure from the monks, rigorous daily routines. This unique asceticism, however, also proved to be the genesis of Shaolin Kung Fu.

As the centuries passed, many subsequent masters contributed to this core of exercises until it developed into a comprehensive system that promoted not only vigorous health but also self-defense. During the Ming Dynasty, a layman entered the Shaolin order: his name was Kwok Yuen, and he dreamed of furthering the knowledge and prestige of Shaolin Kung Fu. With this task in mind he left the Temple seeking to train with as many famed masters as he could find outside the monastery walls. One day he happened upon an old man who was being accosted by some young ruffians; Kwok Yuen thought to intervene and help the old man, but before he could do anything, the old man burst out in a flurry of martial techniques and, to his amazement, easily subdued the assailants.

Greatly impressed, the Shaolin monk inquired how the old man could have fought so well. The old man said his name was Li Chueng and his skill at Kung Fu was not much at all, but his friend's was much better. Without further delay Kwok Yuen asked to be taken to him. The other master was Bak Yuen Fung, and together the three went back to the Temple to begin the task of raising the caliber of Shaolin Kung Fu.

The three masters labored to help the already existing set of techniques evolve by drawing inspiration from animals and nature. They finally settled on compiling the best techniques from five different animals to make the foundation of their new Kung Fu system.

The Five Animal System of Kung Fu is comprised of the Dragon, Snake, Tiger, Leopard, and Crane. Each of these animals is an independent style unto itself. In this book we will look at the techniques of the tiger and its method of attack and defense.

虎形拳 TIGER FORM

The tiger form is one of the classical animal forms of the five animal system of kung fu. The tiger was regarded as a powerful symbol in ancient China, having – it was thought – the sign of "king" written on its head, and thus the tiger is the king of all beasts to the Chinese. To this day the tiger is still revered as a sort of demigod protector and dispeller of evil and bad omens.

The two unique tiger forms and their corresponding matching set presented in this book are a compilation based on the skills and knowledge my teacher gave me and reflect my personal approach to training and utilizing the techniques of the tiger form of kung fu. Training in the tiger form embodies sheer physical power and ferocity, yet balanced with grace and proportion. As so aptly captured by the famous poet William Blake in "*The Tyger*," the tiger form is a "frame" for "fearful symmetry."

Training in the tiger form is meant to strengthen the bones, muscles, and tissues of the body, and to bestow upon the practitioner the tiger's attitude, mentality, and physical prowess because it is patterned after the attributes of the great cat. Pouncing, leaping, clawing, striking, trapping, and kicking are just some of the techniques used in the tiger form to emulate the fighting style of this noble beast. In the tiger form all parts of the body may be used as a weapon, an idea epitomized by its utilizing the entire body behind every movement with power and grace.

Tiger Claw Block in Cross Stance
The attacking attitude of the tiger is infused into every movement of the tiger form.

Trapping Hands in Bow Stance
A combination of strong stances and clawing techniques are a hallmark of the tiger form.

Tiger Claw Mirror Hand in Horse Stance
The tiger's posture is always ready to attack, his gaze fixed upon his prey.

1. Ready position, fist at waist.

2. Palms pressing down, sink breath.

5. Bring hands to waist in double palm block.

6. Double elbow striking upward.

3. Raise up both hands in mirror hand position.

4. Dynamic palm press, execute 3 times.

7. Bring hands to waist in double palm block.

8. Double finger strike.

9. Sink both arms down into "kiu sao" (bridge hand position).

10. Bow with tiger claw and fist at heart level.

13. Dynamic tiger claw exercise.

14. Dynamic tiger claw exercise.

11. Return hands to ready position.

12. Open horse stance.

15. Dynamic tiger claw exercise.

16. Tiger ready position.

17. Butterfly palm in tiger stance.

18. Right swiping claw in kneeling stance.

21. Right swatting claw in crane stance.

22. Spin around and apply double claw trapping hand in left bow stance.

19. Tiger claw block in cross stance.

20. Two tigers entrapping hands in right bow stance.

23. Sit back into low back stance and pull apart hands with claw.

24. Right crescent kick.

夜虎出林

25. Jump back and assume crane stance with open claw position.

26. Jump forward and execute right claw to groin.

29. Open claws and bring down with dynamic tension.

30. Twist claws outward with dynamic tension.

27. Shift back and tear open with double tiger claw.

28. Sift forward and apply double claw trapping hand in left bow stance

31. Return to horse stance and execute 3 mirror hand blocks. (#31-33)

32.

33.

34. Stand up and press palms down to sink internal energy.

35. Raise hands up in mirror hand position.

36. Draw hands in and perform salutation.

Double Tiger Claw Strike
Both hands simulate the firece attack of a pouncing tiger.

Downward Raking Claw
The tiger form flexes every bit of energy into all its movements.

Single Tiger Claw Strike
Powerful claws ripping and gouging with every attack.

1. Ready position, fist at waist.

2. Palms pressing down, sink breath.

5. Bring hands to waist in double palm block.

6. Double elbow striking upward.

3. Raise up both hands in mirror hand position.

4. Dynamic palm press. (execute 3 times)

夜虎出林

24

7. Bring hands to waist in double palm block.

8. Double finger strike.

9. Sink both arms down into "kiu sao" (bridge hand position).

10. Bow with tiger claw and fist at heart level.

13. Dynamic tiger claw exercise.

14. Dynamic tiger claw exercise.

11. Return hands to ready position.

12. Open horse stance.

15. Dynamic tiger claw exercise.

16. Tiger stance ready position.

17. Single tiger claw in tiger stance.

18. Double tiger claw in bow stance.

21. Claw to groin in kneeling stance.

22. Buddha's palm strike in bow stance.

19. Raking claw in cross stance.

20. Double tiger claw in bow stance.

23. Open claw in crouching stance.

24. 360° leg sweep.

夜虎出林

25. Tiger claw mirror hand in horse stance.

26. Tiger claw x-block in bow stance.

29. Twist claws outward with dynamic tension.

30. Return to horse stance and execute 3 mirror hand blocks. (#30-32)

27. Double tiger claw strike to head.

28. Open claws and bring down with dynamic tension.

31.

32.

33. Stand up and press palms down to sink internal energy.

34. Raise hands up in mirror hand position.

35. Draw hands in and perform salutation.

夜虎出林

夜虎出林　MOONLIGHT TIGER MATCHING SET

The "*Moonlight Tiger*" matching set is a specialized training form used as a means of training in the basic techniques and syntax of the tiger form of kung fu. Prior to training with your partner in the actual matching set it is wise to be well-versed in your particular form; at first do not try to learn both forms, but rather master one at a time before proceeding to the next.

Make sure to have a good grasp of each technique and the posture of both forms; this will expand your knowledge of all the techniques taught in this set, as well as give you a solid foundation for the matching set.

When training the tiger matching set beginning slowly at first is best. Practice one movement at a time with your partner and do not exceed more than three techniques until you have fully grasped their application. As you become more familiar with the set and your partner's counter-techniques you can add on more movements.

Take time and care to review all the steps of the set, coordinate your hands and feet smoothly without trying too hard. As time goes on and you practice more, your movements will naturally become faster and more powerful. Training in the matching set will greatly increase your awareness, timing, focus, and understanding of usage in its respective techniques.

Follow a gradual process in building your endurance and technique; execute the set with proper timing, distance and fluid transition of technique. Remember to keep your stance firm yet flexible, and your hands loose but powerful; move in unison with your training partner.

夜虎出林

Tiger Claw Grasping
Controlling with the tiger claw in a low crouching stance.

Intercepting with the
Butterfly Palm Technique

Applying the **Tiger Claw Trapping Hands.**

1. Sifu and Sihing assume the ready position with feet together and fist drawn to the waist.

3. Raise both arms in a mirror hand position.

2. Execute a sinking palm to the side of the body to sink and concentrate the internal energy.

4. Circle both palms around and execute three dynamic palm pushes from the shoulder.

5. Draw in both palms to the waist.

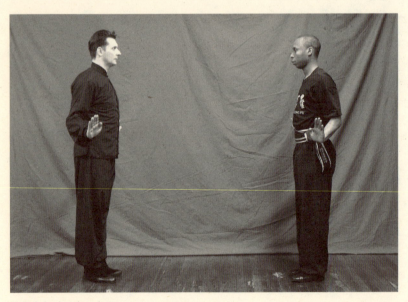
7. Sink both palms down.

6. Execute a rising elbow strike with both hands.

8. Shoot out a finger strike with both hands to the shoulder level.

9. Sink both hands into a firm bridge hand position.

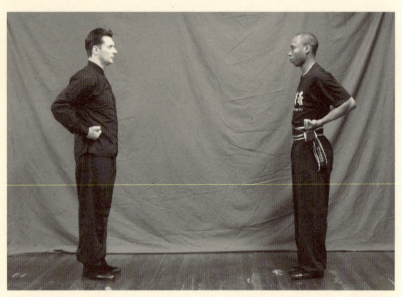
11. Draw both hands back to waist.

10. Bring both hands forward in a circle, right fist, left palm to form the traditional salutation.

12. Open up to horse stance facing your partner.

13. Execute 3 dynamic claw hand strikes to left and right sides. (#13-15)

15.

14.

16. Sifu evades Sihings single tiger claw strike by shifting to a side stance position.

17. Sihing attacks with a double tiger claw strike, Sifu intercepts with a butterfly palm.

19. Sihing counter attacks with a downward claw rake as Sifu blocks with a rising tiger claw in cross stance.

18. Sifu follows through with a claw strike to the groin as Sihing deflects it with a inside leg block.

20. Sifu spins around to escape and traps Sihing's double tiger claw attack .

21. Sifu then counters with a claw swipe to the head as Sihing attacks with claw to groin. Sifu deflects with his foot.

23. Sifu quickly pulls Sihing off balance.

22. Both partners turn around, Sihing attacks with buddha palm strike to throat as Sifu traps with double tiger forearm block.

24. Sifu executes a high inside crescent kick which Sihing evades by ducking down.

25. Immediately Sihing execute a 360° back sweep as Sifu jumps away.

27. Sifu leaps in and attacks groin as Sihing blocks with tiger claw x-block.

26. Both partners assume ready positions.

28. Sifu simultaneously tears off block and traps Sihings' hands.

29. Sihing escapes and attacks with two circular tiger claw strikes to the head as Sifu traps with inside forearm block.

31. Both partners draw back to low tiger claw position.

30. Sifu opens up Sihing with dynamic claw technique blocking downward.

32. Both return to horse stance and execute 3 tiger claw mirror hands with dynamic tension. (#32-34)

33.

35. Both partners execute a sinking palm to the side of the body to sink and concentrate the internal energy.

34

36. Raise both arms in a mirror hand position.

夜虎出林

37. Bring both hands forward in a circle, right fist, left palm to form the traditional salutation.

38. Draw both hands back to waist, end of matching set.

夜虎出林

About the Author

Sifu Paul Koh has been training in the art of Chinese Kung Fu for the past twenty-five years, beginning with the instruction he received from Master Tony Lau and culminating with the instruction he received over the past decade from Master Tak Wah Eng, both of whom were senior students of Grandmaster Wai Hong. Under their tutelage, he has learned a wide variety of Kung Fu styles, including Northern and Southern Shaolin, Five Animal System, and classical weaponry.